MW00436839

_____

To

_____

From

_____

Date

Hold fast your dreams! Within your heart
keep one still, secret spot where dreams may go
and, sheltered so, may thrive and grow.

LOUISE DRISCOLL

■

Delight yourself in the Lord and he will give
you the desires of your heart.... Be still
before the Lord.

PSALM 37:4,7 NIV

■